TABLE OF CONTENTS

Workbook Answers

Chapter 1 - Place Value and Number Sense

Pg 6

Pg 7			
No.	**Answer**	**No.**	**Answer**
1	even	13	odd
2	odd	14	even
3	even	15	even
4	even	16	even
5	odd	17	odd
6	even	18	odd
7	odd	19	even
8	odd	20	even
9	even	21	odd
10	odd	22	odd
11	odd	23	even
12	even	24	even

Pg 8		Pg 9		Pg 10		Pg 11	
No.	Answer	No.	Answer	No.	Answer	No.	Answer
1	odd	1	300	1	8,000	1	78
2	even	2	900	2	1,000	2	34
3	even	3	300	3	2,000	3	15
4	odd	4	100	4	9,000	4	2
5	odd	5	200	5	1,000	5	8
6	even	6	800	6	6,000	6	9
7	odd	7	800	7	4,000	7	3
8	even	8	100	8	9,000	8	5
9	even	9	800	9	2,000	9	89
10	even	10	400	10	7,000		
11	odd	11	300	11	2,000		
12	odd	12	300	12	5,000		
13	even	13	600	13	7,000		
14	odd	14	1,000	14	4,000		
15	odd	15	200	15	7,000		
16	even	16	300	16	9,000		
17	even	17	400	17	1,000		
18	even	18	700	18	5,000		
19	even	19	700	19	5,000		
20	even	20	500	20	2,000		
21	odd	21	200	21	2,000		
22	odd	22	800	22	1,000		
23	odd	23	300	23	2,000		
24	even	24	200	24	5,000		
		25	800	25	1,000		
		26	200	26	9,000		
		27	800	27	8,000		
		28	300	28	3,000		

Pg 12		Pg 13		Pg 14	
No.	Answer	No.	Answer	No.	Answer
1	24	1	129	1	1,347
2	43	2	235	2	3,232
3	39	3	254	3	2,459
4	66	4	325	4	4,157
5	59	5	507	5	3,175
6	86				

<table>
<tr><th colspan="2">Pg 15</th></tr>
<tr><th>No.</th><th>Answer</th></tr>
<tr><td>1</td><td>4,818 | 4,982 | 14,818</td></tr>
<tr><td>2</td><td>880 | 1,251 |1,900</td></tr>
<tr><td>3</td><td>1,210 | 1,541 | 1,780</td></tr>
<tr><td>4</td><td>50 | 74 | 129</td></tr>
<tr><td>5</td><td>815 | 1,520 | 3,500</td></tr>
<tr><td>6</td><td>3,400 | 5,800 | 9,570</td></tr>
<tr><td>7</td><td>10 | 100 | 1,000</td></tr>
<tr><td>8</td><td>5 | 300 | 4,500</td></tr>
<tr><td>9</td><td>250 | 275 | 300</td></tr>
<tr><td>10</td><td>16 | 25 | 54</td></tr>
</table>

Pg 16		Pg 17		Pg 18	
No.	**Answer**	**No.**	**Answer**	**No.**	**Answer**
1	>	1	>	1	1,221
2	>	2	<	2	2,142
3	<	3	=	3	333
4	<	4	>	4	3,321
5	<	5	>	5	2,340
6	=	6	>		
7	=	7	<		
8	<	8	<		
9	>	9	=		
10	<	10	<		
11	>	11	>		
12	<	12	<		
13	>	13	>		
14	=	14	=		
15	>	15	<		
16	>	16	<		
17	<	17	=		
18	=	18	>		
19	<	19	>		
20	<	20	<		

Pg 19

The place value of a digit is determined by where it is in a number.

Hundred Thousands	Ten Thousands	Thousands	Hundreds	Tens	Ones
1	2	3	4	5	6

123,456

One Hundred Twenty Three Thousand, Four Hundred Fifty Six

Write these numbers correctly in the blanks.

1. 392,599 =

3	9	2	5	9	9
Hundred Thousands	Ten Thousands	Thousands	Hundreds	Tens	Ones

2. 415,675 =

4	1	5	6	7	5
Hundred Thousands	Ten Thousands	Thousands	Hundreds	Tens	Ones

3. 726,211 =

7	2	6	2	1	1
Hundred Thousands	Ten Thousands	Thousands	Hundreds	Tens	Ones

4. 186,452 =

1	8	6	4	5	2
Hundred Thousands	Ten Thousands	Thousands	Hundreds	Tens	Ones

Chapter 2 – Addition

Pg 21		Pg 22		Pg 23	
No.	**Answer**	**No.**	**Answer**	**No.**	**Answer**
1	79	1	121	1	166
2	89	2	47	2	134
3	62	3	89	3	138
4	77	4	84	4	131
5	99	5	113	5	55
6	106	6	94	6	165
7	78	7	42	7	44
8	38	8	116	8	151
9	69	9	86	9	113
10	78	10	23	10	87
11	29	11	88	11	120
12	47	12	53	12	125
		13	91	13	84
		14	87	14	105
		15	128	15	25
		16	119	16	97
		17	86	17	60
		18	78	18	60
		19	120	19	77

Pg 24	
No.	**Answer**
1	100 + 10 + 10 + 1 = 121
2	100 + 1 + 1 + 1 + 1 + 1 = 105
3	100 + 100 + 100 + 100 + 100 + 10 = 510
4	10 + 10 + 10 + 10 + 1 + 1 = 42
5	100 + 100 + 10 + 10 + 10 + 10 = 240
6	100 + 10 + 1 + 1 + 1 +1 = 114
7	100 + 100 + 100 + 10 + 1 + 1 = 312
8	100 + 10 + 10 + 10 +10 + 1 = 141

Pg 25	
No.	**Answer**
1	1,000 + 100 + 10 + 1 + 1 = 1,112
2	1,000 + 1,000 + 1,000 + 100 + 1 = 3,101
3	1,000 + 100 + 100 + 10 + 1 + 1 = 1,212
4	1,000 + 1,000 + 1,000 + 1,000 + 100 = 4,100
5	1,000 + 1,000 + 100 + 100 + 10 + 10 = 2,220
6	100 + 10 + 10 + 1 + 1 + 1 = 123
7	1,000 + 1,000 + 100 + 10 + 10 + 1 = 2,121
8	100 + 100 + 100 + 10 + 10 + 1 = 321

Pg 26		Pg 27		Pg 28	
No.	**Answer**	**No.**	**Answer**	**No.**	**Answer**
1	1,806	1	1,773	1	2,387
2	892	2	2,782	2	1,190
3	1,330	3	851	3	3,055
4	923	4	1,437	4	2,254
5	1,322	5	1,648	5	1,569
6	831	6	1,286	6	2,266
7	389	7	899	7	1,619
8	1,054	8	1,208	8	2,094
9	1,580	9	2,228	9	1,536
10	204	10	1,511	10	2,321
11	964	11	1,054	11	1,485
12	876	12	1,947	12	1,481
13	1,364	13	1,673	13	1,038
14	648	14	1,395	14	1,833
15	714	15	722	15	1,182
16	1,030				
17	1,046				
18	562				
19	975				

Pg 29

Fill in the blanks to complete each problem.

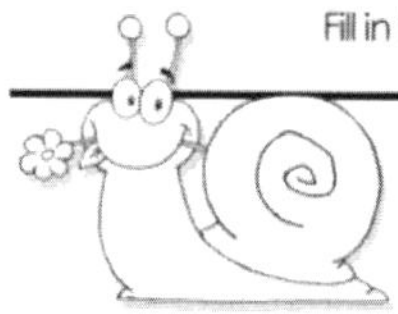

1. 124 + 191 = 315
2. 239 + 632 = 871
3. 348 + 631 = 979
4. 623 + 222 = 845
5. 137 + 447 = 584
6. 583 + 391 = 974
7. 375 + 175 = 550
8. 115 + 122 = 237
9. 424 + 123 = 547
10. 524 + 261 = 785
11. 234 + 162 = 396

Pg 30		Pg 31	
No.	Answer	No.	Answer
1	5,501	1	7,641
2	7,061	2	10,626
3	8,636	3	11,044
4	8,023	4	21,672
5	8,711	5	19,295
6	9,482	6	22,701
7	4,121	7	19,214
8	15,195	8	23,256
9	18,911	9	18,628
10	6,526	10	11,171
11	14,723	11	9,686
12	8,041	12	21,667
13	7,905		
14	10,164		
15	4,399		

Pg 32

- Add the numbers going down
- Add the numbers going across.
- Then add your answers together, either across or down, to fill in the the last square

3	4	7
2	3	5
5	7	(12)

1.

1	5	6
5	2	7
6	7	(13)

2.

2	8	10
8	9	17
10	17	(27)

3.

6	3	9
3	6	9
9	9	(18)

4.

2	15	17
15	2	17
17	17	(34)

5.

25	4	29
4	10	14
29	14	(43)

6.

1	8	9
8	40	48
9	48	(57)

Pg 33

- Add the numbers going down
- Add the numbers going across.
- Then add your answers together, either across or down, to fill in the the last square

3	4	7
2	3	5
5	7	(12)

1.

10	3	13
3	10	13
13	13	(26)

2.

5	8	13
8	5	13
13	13	(26)

3.

1	7	8
7	1	8
8	8	(16)

4.

3	6	9
6	12	18
9	18	(27)

5.

70	13	83
13	45	58
83	58	(141)

6.

2	36	38
36	2	38
38	38	(76)

Chapter 3 – Subtraction

Pg 35		Pg 36		Pg 37		Pg 38	
No.	**Answer**	**No.**	**Answer**	**No.**	**Answer**	**No.**	**Answer**
1	13	1	2	1	44	1	28
2	5	2	7	2	45	2	37
3	5	3	7	3	23	3	66
4	36	4	4	4	8	4	42
5	37	5	53	5	23	5	526
6	20	6	61	6	55	6	612
7	22	7	6	7	9	7	523
8	22	8	48	8	8	8	472
9	27	9	68	9	52	9	678
10	14	10	40	10	41	10	378
11	59	11	8	11	33	11	65
12	43	12	60	12	36	12	605
		13	35	13	28	13	341
		14	48	14	61	14	483
		15	17	15	35	15	157
		16	8	16	55	16	77
		17	36	17	2	17	361
		18	31	18	18	18	313
		19	14	19	30	19	87

Pg 39		Pg 40		Pg 41		Pg 42	
No.	**Answer**	**No.**	**Answer**	**No.**	**Answer**	**No.**	**Answer**
1	380	1	182	1	85	1	105
2	658	2	119	2	32	2	80
3	204	3	299	3	136	3	170
4	261	4	106	4	42	4	30
5	457	5	87	5	81	5	135
6	3	6	156	6	53	6	20
7	204	7	155	7	83	7	119
8	277	8	260	8	73	8	199
9	339	9	77	9	112	9	41
10	769	10	110	10	74	10	86
11	359	11	425	11	20	11	50
12	338	12	55	12	61	12	40
13	551	13	208	13	37	13	60
14	249	14	234	14	160	14	15
15	769	15	23	15	40	15	30
16	555	16	236	16	57	16	30
17	520	17	502	17	92	17	187
18	166	18	592	18	16	18	75
19	794	19	104	19	356	19	180
				20	30	20	161

Pg 43		Pg 44		Pg 45		Pg 46	
No.	Answer	No.	Answer	No.	Answer	No.	Answer
1	194	1	2,071	1	3,366	1	1,889
2	591	2	2,009	2	904	2	4,267
3	122	3	8,920	3	2,459	3	1,044
4	793	4	2,980	4	154	4	2,589
5	377	5	3,331	5	861	5	3,679
6	881	6	4,091	6	1,248	6	19
7	587	7	5,071	7	3,761	7	889
8	314	8	4,334	8	3,626	8	489
9	233	9	2,781	9	5,071	9	1,175
10	195	10	5,565	10	1,925	10	2,689
11	619	11	7,573	11	2,075	11	1,230
12	214	12	1,121	12	111	12	6,495
13	55	13	1,213	13	3,454	13	3,353
14	66	14	1,151	14	320	14	3,984
15	378						
16	46						
17	473						
18	95						
19	66						

Pg 47	
No.	Answer
1	4,690
2	5,844
3	2,045
4	2,571
5	1,784
6	4,222
7	5,406
8	5,897
9	6,122
10	5,009
11	5,329
12	408
13	9,036
14	676

Chapter 4 - Division

Pg 50

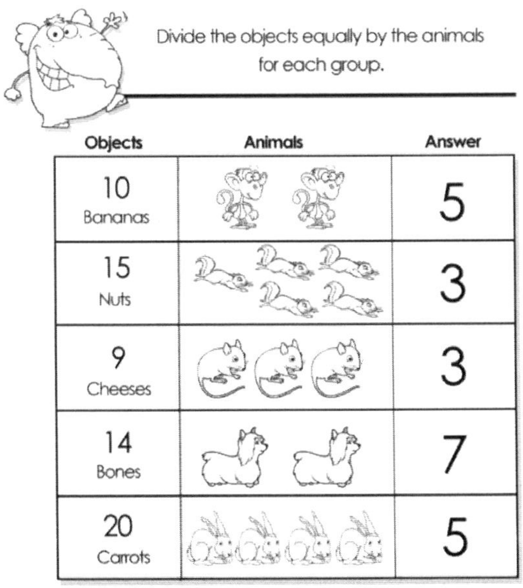

Divide the objects equally by the animals for each group.

Objects	Animals	Answer
10 Bananas		5
15 Nuts		3
9 Cheeses		3
14 Bones		7
20 Carrots		5

Pg 51

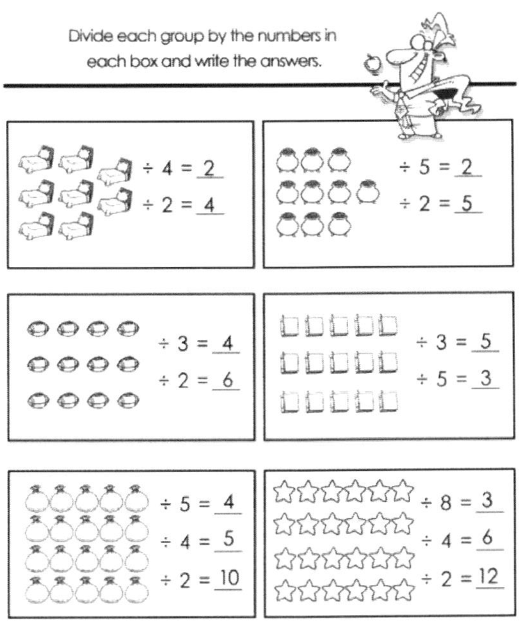

Divide each group by the numbers in each box and write the answers.

$\div 4 = 2$
$\div 2 = 4$

$\div 5 = 2$
$\div 2 = 5$

$\div 3 = 4$
$\div 2 = 6$

$\div 3 = 5$
$\div 5 = 3$

$\div 5 = 4$
$\div 4 = 5$
$\div 2 = 10$

$\div 8 = 3$
$\div 4 = 6$
$\div 2 = 12$

Pg 52	
No.	Answer
1	18, 9, 2
2	16, 4, 4
3	125, 5, 25
4	15, 3, 5
5	100, 10, 10
6	72, 9, 8
7	4, 12, 3
8	5, 30, 6
9	6, 42, 7
10	8, 64, 8
11	2, 10, 5
12	3, 21, 7

Pg 53		Pg 54		Pg 55	
No.	Answer	No.	Answer	No.	Answer
1	7	1	24 ÷ 8 = 3, 24 ÷ 6 = 4	1	6
2	7	2	15 ÷ 3 = 5, 15 ÷ 5 = 3	2	5
3	46	3	10 ÷ 2 = 5, 10 ÷ 5 = 2	3	6
4	52	4	50 ÷ 5 = 10, 50 ÷ 10 = 5	4	4
5	28			5	4
6	37			6	9
7	27			7	8
8	33			8	9
9	22			9	8
10	99			10	8
11	59				
12	82				
13	80				
14	90				
15	30				
16	97				
17	46				
18	95				
19	59				
20	65				

Pg 56		Pg 57		Pg 58		Pg 59	
No.	**Answer**	**No.**	**Answer**	**No.**	**Answer**	**No.**	**Answer**
1	10	1	20	1	8	1	14
2	4	2	4	2	18	2	5
3	5	3	25	3	10	3	7
4	5	4	15	4	6	4	10
5	7	5	6	5	3	5	7
6	1	6	10	6	4	6	9
7	5	7	5	7	2	7	18
8	10	8	25	8	10	8	10
9	3	9	19	9	7	9	5
10	6	10	12	10	5	10	4
		11	22	11	17	11	36
		12	30	12	6	12	6
		13	10	13	13	13	10
		14	42	14	18	14	36
		15	6	15	21	15	5
		16	18	16	40	16	7
						17	100
						18	10
						19	40
						20	15

Pg 60	
No.	**Answer**
1	30
2	5
3	63
4	29
5	2
6	7
7	48
8	5
9	4
10	3
11	92
12	9
13	10
14	55
15	6
16	8
17	22
18	7
19	14
20	16

Chapter 5 – Fractions

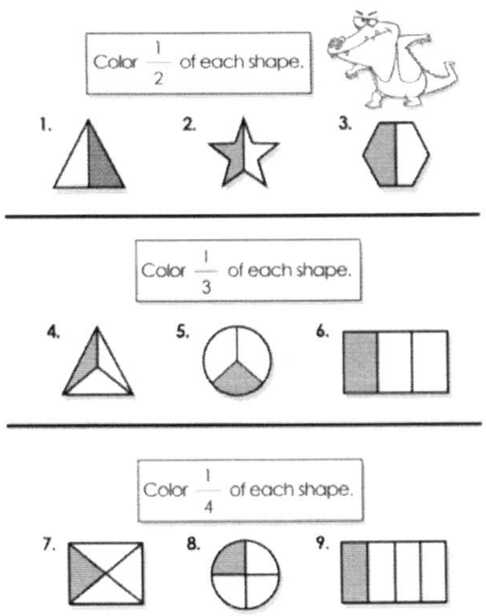

Pg 63

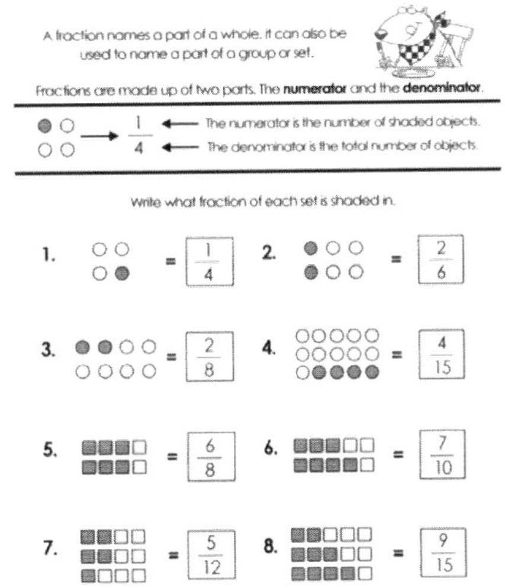

Pg 64

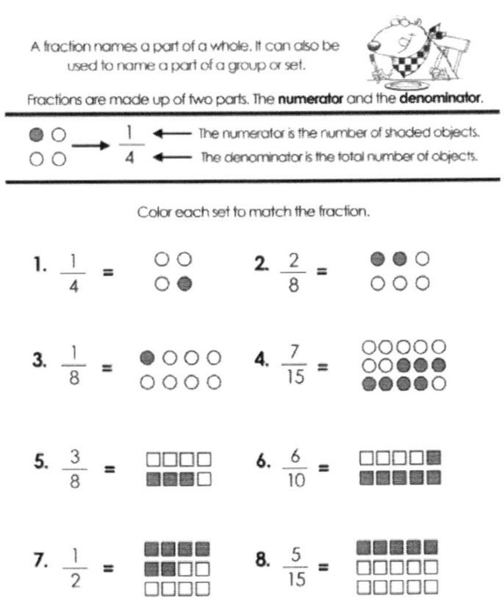

Pg 65

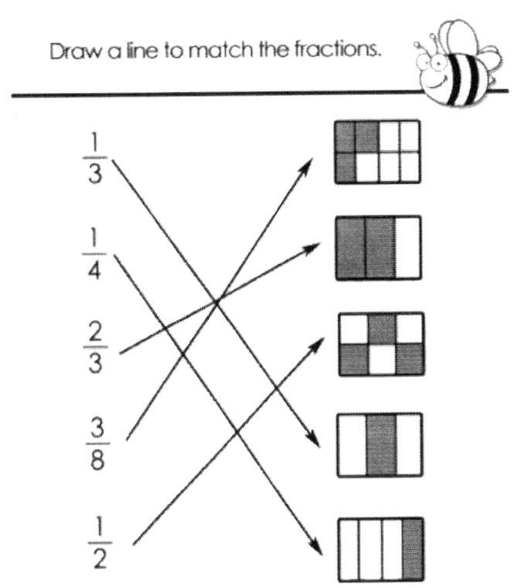

Pg 66

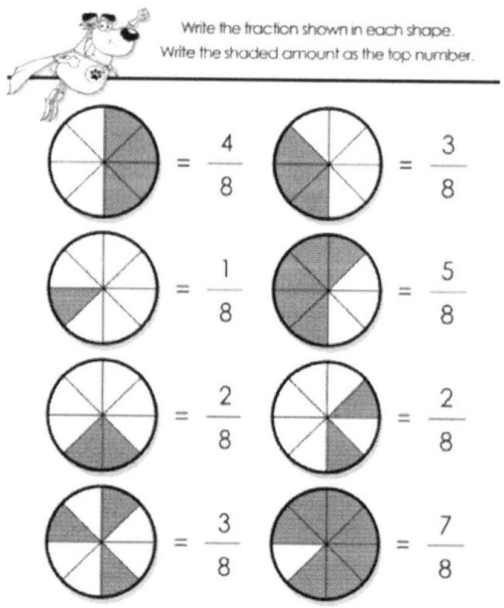

Pg 67

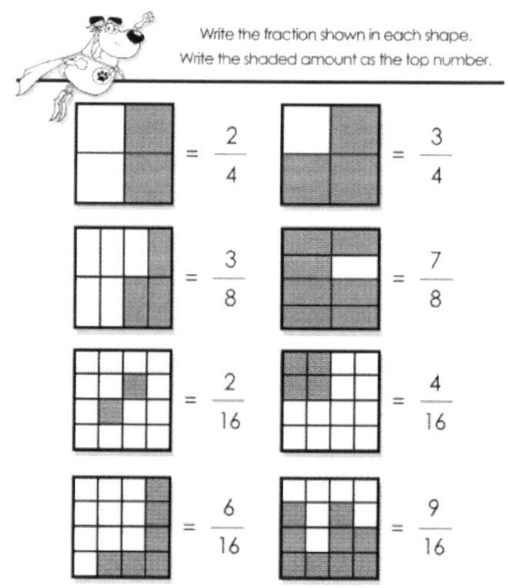

Pg 68

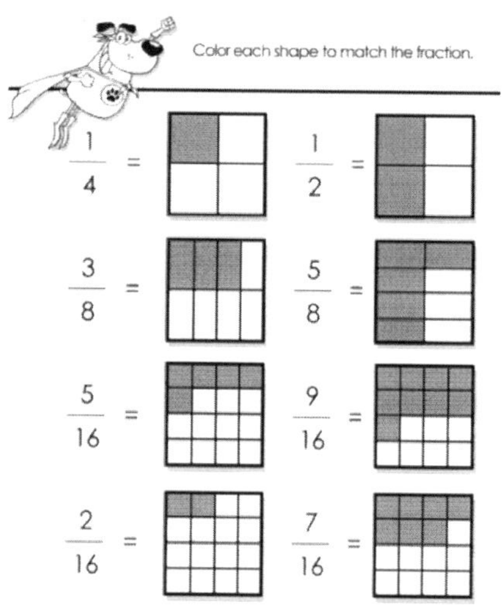

Pg 69

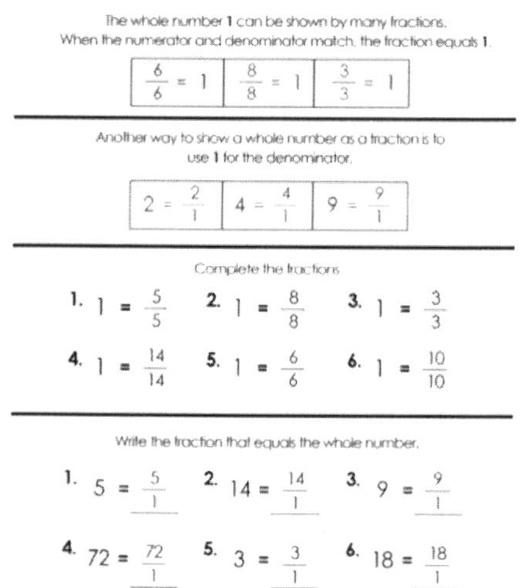
The whole number **1** can be shown by many fractions.
When the numerator and denominator match, the fraction equals **1**.

$\frac{6}{6} = 1$	$\frac{8}{8} = 1$	$\frac{3}{3} = 1$

Another way to show a whole number as a fraction is to use **1** for the denominator.

$2 = \frac{2}{1}$	$4 = \frac{4}{1}$	$9 = \frac{9}{1}$

Complete the fractions

1. $1 = \frac{5}{5}$ **2.** $1 = \frac{8}{8}$ **3.** $1 = \frac{3}{3}$

4. $1 = \frac{14}{14}$ **5.** $1 = \frac{6}{6}$ **6.** $1 = \frac{10}{10}$

Write the fraction that equals the whole number.

1. $5 = \frac{5}{1}$ **2.** $14 = \frac{14}{1}$ **3.** $9 = \frac{9}{1}$

4. $72 = \frac{72}{1}$ **5.** $3 = \frac{3}{1}$ **6.** $18 = \frac{18}{1}$

Pg 70

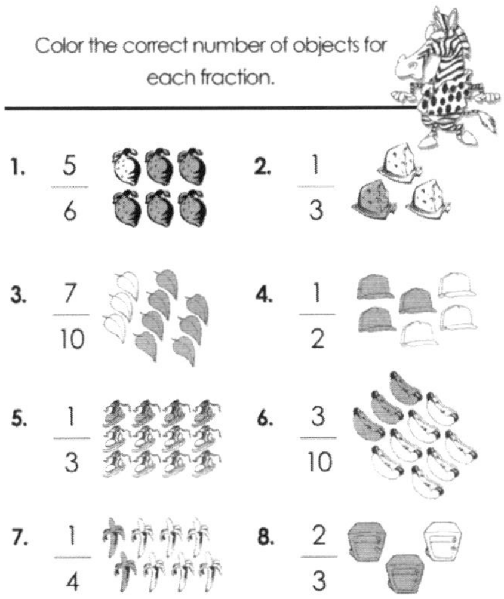

Pg 71

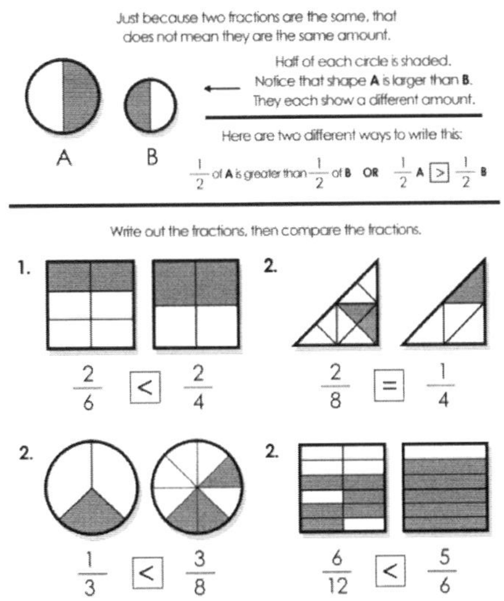

Pg 72

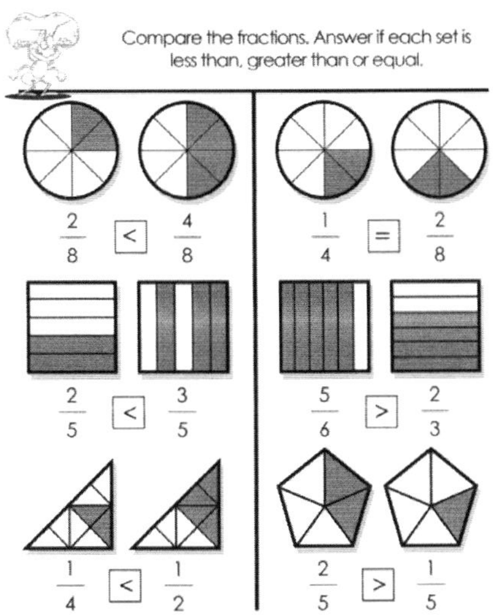

Pg 73

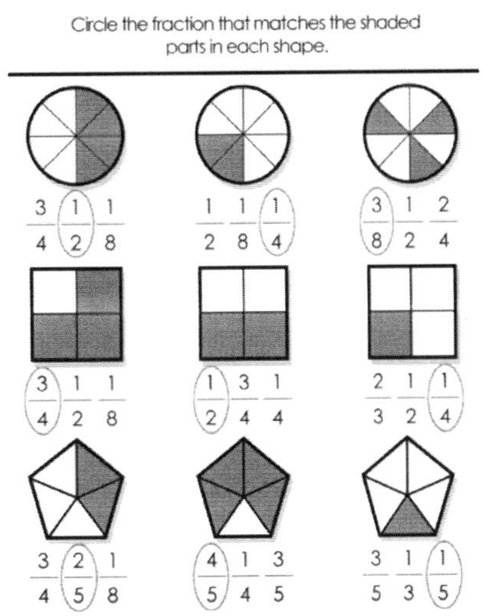

Pg 74

Chapter 6 – Multiplication

Pg 76

Multiplication is the way we find the sum of the same number a certain amount of times.

4 x 2 = 8
2 + 2 + 2 + 2 = 8
□□ □□ □□ □□

2 x 5 = 10
5 + 5 = 10
□□ □□
□□ □□
□ □

Break each group down by writing them out, then adding them together.

1. 3 x 2 = 6
2 + 2 + 2 = 6

2. 3 x 4 = 12
4 + 4 + 4 = 12

3. 4 x 4 = 16
4 + 4 + 4 + 4 = 16

4. 4 x 5 = 20
5 + 5 + 5 + 5 = 20

5. 3 x 8 = 24
8 + 8 + 8 = 24

6. 4 x 10 = 40
10 + 10 + 10 + 10 = 40

5. 2 x 6 = 12
6 + 6 = 12

6. 3 x 6 = 18
6 + 6 + 6 = 18

Pg 77			
No.	**Answer**	**No.**	**Answer**
1	0	12	4
2	4	13	6
3	1	14	5
4	9	15	3
5	9	16	0
6	6	17	2
7	2	18	7
8	8	19	8
9	6	20	7
10	0	21	0
11	3		

Pg 78		Pg 79		Pg 80		Pg 81	
No.	**Answer**	**No.**	**Answer**	**No.**	**Answer**	**No.**	**Answer**
1	18	1	6	1	3	1	12
2	8	2	0	2	0	2	10
3	16	3	4	3	20	3	35
4	7	4	14	4	12	4	18
5	18	5	24	5	4	5	0
6	10	6	12	6	16	6	5
7	7	7	18	7	0	7	18
8	4	8	24	8	28	8	40
9	6	9	0	9	8	9	0
10	6	10	16	10	2	10	16
11	18	11	27	11	36	11	30
12	8	12	21	12	20	12	25
13	14	13	0	13	32	13	4
14	10	14	9	14	4	14	45
15	0	15	2	15	0	15	18
16	12	16	7	16	24	16	16
17	16	17	0	17	18	17	0
18	0	18	15	18	27	18	15
19	4	19	9	19	12	19	9
20	2	20	15	20	12	20	10
21	8	21	18	21	27	21	18

Pg 82		Pg 83		Pg 84		Pg 85	
No.	**Answer**	**No.**	**Answer**	**No.**	**Answer**	**No.**	**Answer**
1	0	1	12	1	56	1	9
2	54	2	0	2	16	2	36
3	15	3	20	3	8	3	56
4	8	4	3	4	12	4	81
5	12	5	42	5	0	5	21
6	6	6	14	6	35	6	40
7	14	7	9	7	72	7	9
8	18	8	21	8	15	8	3
9	36	9	63	9	24	9	24
10	4	10	24	10	0	10	2
11	30	11	28	11	16	11	54
12	24	12	30	12	25	12	16
13	0	13	4	13	16	13	35
14	25	14	35	14	56	14	45
15	27	15	14	15	40	15	36
16	12	16	42	16	72	16	36
17	30	17	7	17	64	17	0
18	15	18	49	18	32	18	18
19	48	19	56	19	32	19	21
20	42	20	7	20	10	20	10
21	0	21	42	21	24	21	27

Pg 86		Pg 87		Pg 88		Pg 89	
No.	**Answer**	**No.**	**Answer**	**No.**	**Answer**	**No.**	**Answer**
1	3	1	30	1	400	1	48
2	4	2	20	2	200	2	219
3	5	3	50	3	500	3	120
4	9	4	60	4	600	4	128
5	6	5	10	5	100	5	48
6	2	6	50	6	400	6	63
7	10	7	40	7	800	7	75
8	8	8	80	8	900	8	108
9	6	9	70	9	0	9	49
10	7	10	0	10	700	10	76
		11	90	11	300		
		12	20	12	700		
		13	40	13	400		
		14	30	14	300		
		15	90	15	900		

Chapter 7 – Graphing

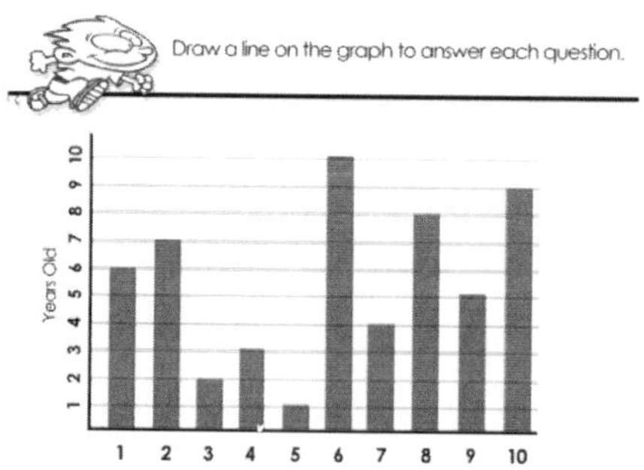
Draw a line on the graph to answer each question.

1. Tom is six years old.
2. Laney is seven years old.
3. Jane is two years old.
4. Stan is three years old.
5. Sally is one year old.
6. Mark is ten years old.
7. Mike is four years old.
8. Anne is eight years old.
9. Elle is five years old.
10. Donnie is nine years old.

Pg 91

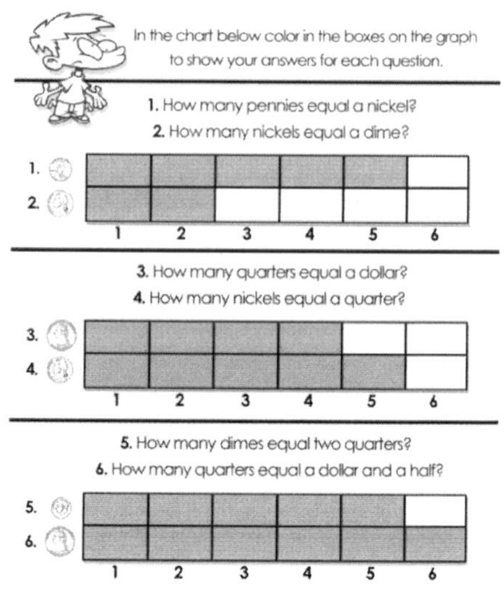
In the chart below color in the boxes on the graph to show your answers for each question.

1. How many pennies equal a nickel?
2. How many nickels equal a dime?

3. How many quarters equal a dollar?
4. How many nickels equal a quarter?

5. How many dimes equal two quarters?
6. How many quarters equal a dollar and a half?

Pg 92

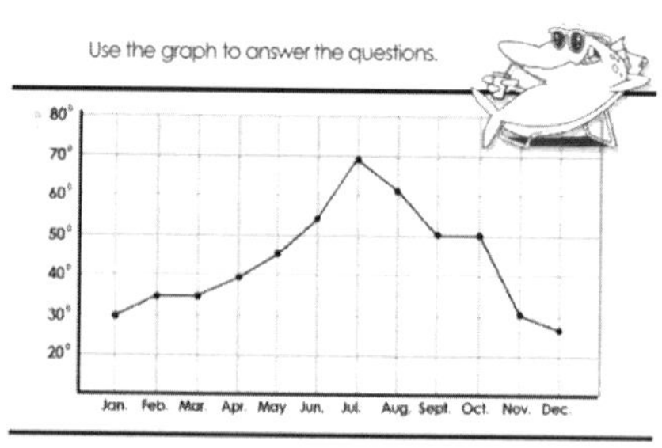
Use the graph to answer the questions.

1. What was the coldest month? December
2. What was the hottest month? July
3. What was the temperature in March? 35 degrees
4. About how many degrees was the difference between the coldest and hottest months? 40-45 degrees
5. What was the temperature in November? 30 degrees
6. Did it become hotter or colder from April to May? hotter
7. Did the temperature change from September to October? no
8. Which month was colder, January or December? December

Pg 93

Pg 95	
No.	**Answer**
1	pancakes
2	ham
3	bacon
4	ham
5	bacon
6	pancakes
7	eggs

Pg 96

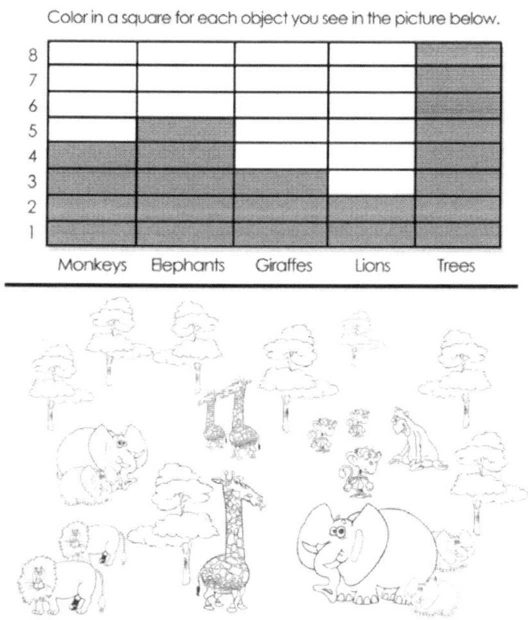

Pg 97		Pg 98	
No.	**Answer**	**No.**	**Answer**
1	3	1	$50
2	5	2	13 miles
3	2	3	32 pieces of candy
4	4	4	97 cupcakes
5	5		
6	1		
7	6		

Pg 99

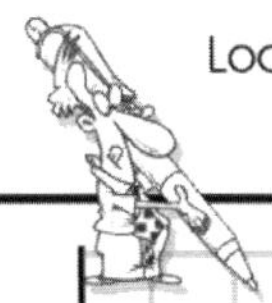

Locate the points on the grid and draw the shapes for each question.

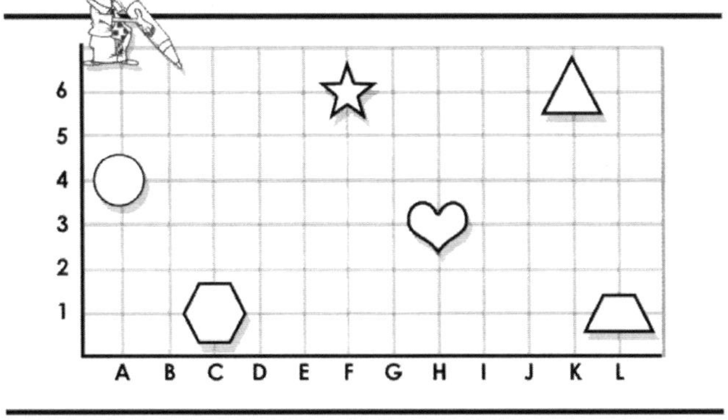

1. A, 4 - 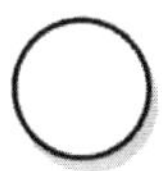
2. C, 1 - 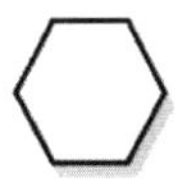
3. K, 6 - 
4. H, 3 - 
5. F, 6 - 
6. L, 1 - 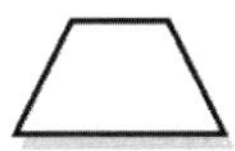

Chapter 8 - Money & Time

Pg 103		Pg 104		Pg 105		Pg 106	
No.	Answer	No.	Answer	No.	Answer	No.	Answer
1	76¢	1	$1.41	1	25¢	1	$3.95
2	72¢	2	$3.12	2	23¢	2	$2.39
3	$1.55	3	$7.61	3	36¢	3	$1.68
4	$1.86	4	$30.18	4	52¢	4	$4.39
5	93¢	5	$25.87	5	$3.93	5	$3.91
6	$1.81	6	$35.33	6	$3.64	6	$6.79
7	$1.36			7	$4.36	7	$9.19
8	$1.09					8	$13.20
9	$1.45						

Pg 107	
No.	Answer
1	thirty-eight dollars and fifty-nine cents
2	one-hundred dollars and thirty-two cents
3	two-hundred seventy-eight dollars and twelve cents
4	three-hundred fifteen dollars and eight cents
5	nine-hundred fifteen dollars and eighty-three cents
6	eighteen dollars and thirty-three cents
7	two-hundred twenty-nine dollars and twenty-nine cents
8	seven-hundred fifty-six dollars and ten cents
9	six-hundred eighteen dollars and twenty-four cents
10	nine-hundred ninety-nine dollars and seventy-two cents

Pg 109

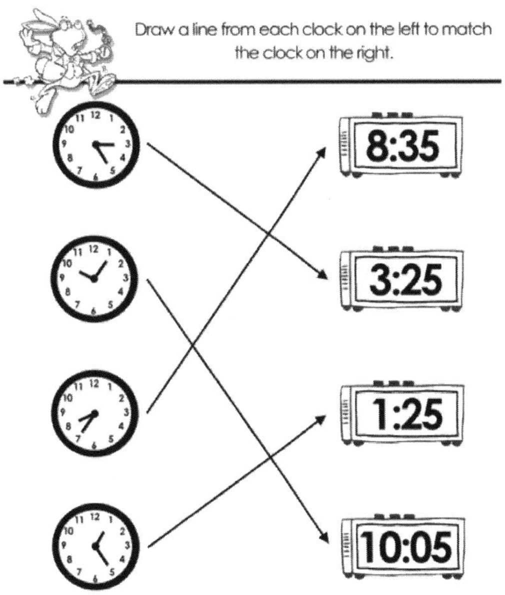

Pg 110		Pg 111	
No.	**Answer**	**No.**	**Answer**
1	AM	1	6 hours 45 minutes
2	PM	2	9 hours 26 minutes
3	AM	3	5 hours 12 minutes
4	PM	4	15 hours 52 minutes
5	PM	5	3 hours 45 minutes
6	AM	6	1 hour 54 minutes
7	PM	7	58 minutes
8	PM	8	3 hours 48 minutes
9	AM		
10	PM		

Pg 112

Write the correct times in the clocks on the right.
9:15
What time will it be in 3 hours and 15 minutes?
10:30
What time will it be in 2 hours and 30 minutes?
12:15
What time will it be in 1 hour and 45 minutes?
4:45
What time will it be in 2 hours and 15 minutes?
5:15
What time will it be in 4 hours and 45 minutes?
8:45
What time will it be in 3 hours and 30 minutes?
8:45
What time will it be in 5 hours and 45 minutes?
9:45
What time will it be in 1 hour and 15 minutes?

Pg 113

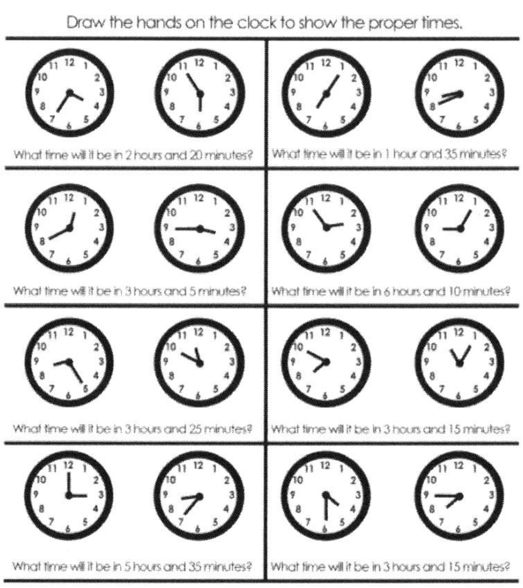
Draw the hands on the clock to show the proper times.
What time will it be in 2 hours and 20 minutes?
What time will it be in 1 hour and 35 minutes?
What time will it be in 3 hours and 5 minutes?
What time will it be in 6 hours and 10 minutes?
What time will it be in 3 hours and 25 minutes?
What time will it be in 3 hours and 15 minutes?
What time will it be in 5 hours and 35 minutes?
What time will it be in 3 hours and 15 minutes?

Chapter 9 - Geometry & Measurements

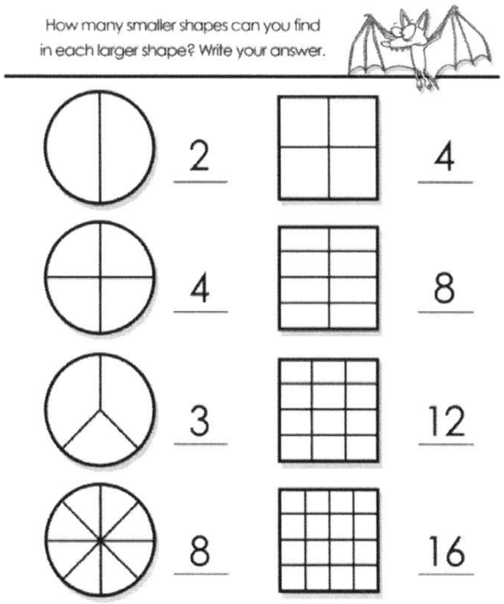

Pg 116

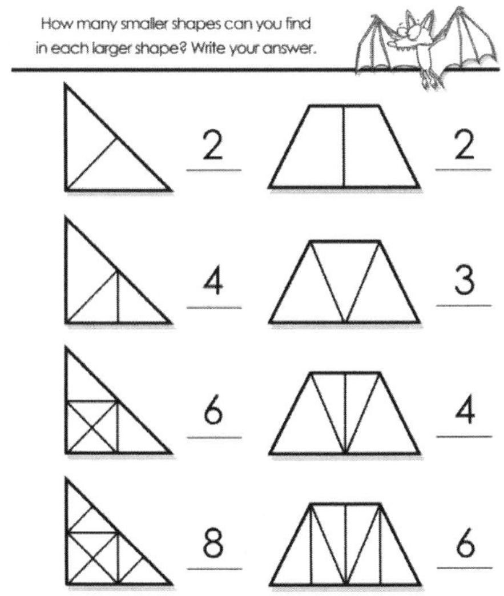

Pg 117

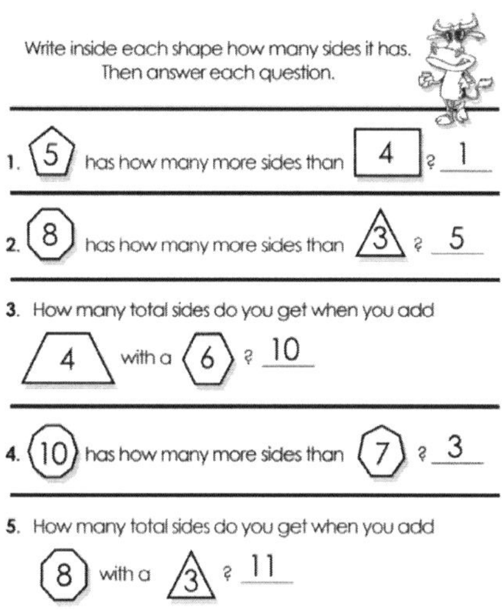

Pg 118

Pg 119	
No.	**Answer**
1	3
2	4
3	6
4	7
5	4
6	7
7	7
8	6

Pg 120

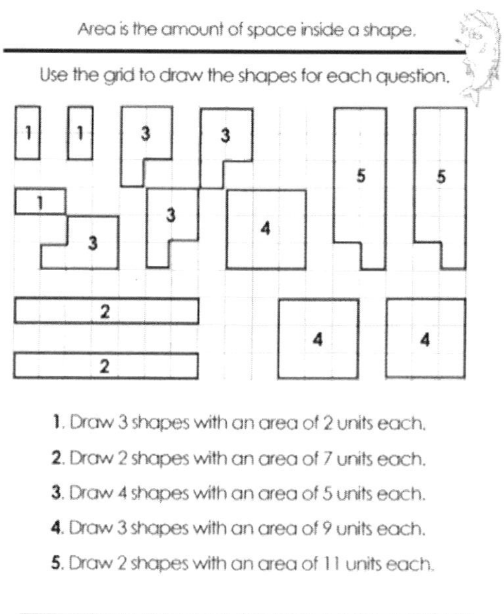

Pg 121		Pg 122	
No.	**Answer**	**No.**	**Answer**
1	4 + 6 + 4 +6 = 20 in	1	8
2	7 + 7 + 7 = 21ft	2	10
3	8 + 20 + 20 + 26 = 74in	3	9
4	12 + 8 + 12 + 8 = 40ft	4	12
5	6 + 6 + 9 +6 + 9 = 36in	5	10
6	3 + 3 + 3 + 3 + 3 + 3 = 18ft	6	12
		7	14
		8	14

Pg 123
Answers can vary

Perimeter is the distance around a two-dimensional shape.

Use the grid to draw the shapes for each question.

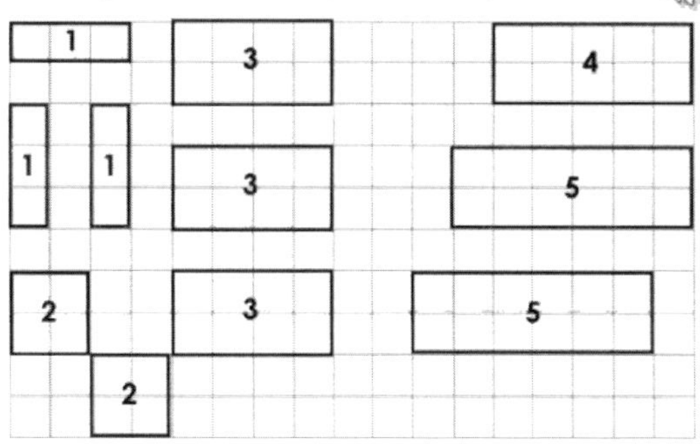

1. Draw 3 shapes with a perimeter of 8 units each.
2. Draw 2 shapes with a perimeter of 20 units each.
3. Draw 3 shapes with a perimeter of 12 units each.
4. Draw 1 shapes with a perimeter of 14 units each.
5. Draw 2 shapes with a perimeter of 16 units each.

Pg 124			
No.	**Answer**	**No.**	**Answer**
1	line segment	1	XY or DF
2	point	2	line segment
3	line	3	any point on the illustration
4	line segment	4	line
		5	E

Pg 125		Pg 126		Pg 127		Pg 128	
No.	**Answer**	**No.**	**Answer**	**No.**	**Answer**	**No.**	**Answer**
1	obtuse	1	Ounces	1	yards	1	cup
2	acute	2	Pounds	2	feet	2	gallon
3	right	3	Ounces	3	miles	3	pint
4	obtuse	4	Pounds	4	feet	4	quart
		5	Pounds	5	feet	5	pint
		6	Ounces	6	miles	6	gallon
				7	feet		
				8	yards		
				9	miles		
				10	foot		

Practice Test Answers

Practice Test #1

Answers and Explanations

1. B: The number, 860,002 has an 8 in the hundred-thousands place, a 6 in the ten-thousands place, a 0 in the thousands place, a 0 in the hundreds place, a 0 in the tens place, and a 2 in the ones place. The 860 written in front of the comma represents, "Eight hundred sixty thousand." The 2 in the ones place represents, "Two." Therefore, the number is read, "Eight hundred sixty thousand, two."

2. D: The annual expenses for Years 2009, 2007, 2008, 2011, and 2010 are \$1,046, \$1,224, \$1,319, \$1,342, and \$1,529, respectively. These amounts are listed in order from lowest to highest. Since all of the numbers have a 1 in the thousands place, the numerals in the hundreds place must be compared. For the amounts of \$1,319 and \$1,342, the numerals in the tens place must be compared. No other choice shows the years listed in increasing order of expense.

3. C: There are 2 dollar bills, which represent 2 dollars. There are also 2 quarters, 2 nickels, 1 dime, and 4 pennies. Two quarters are worth \$0.50 since each is worth \$0.25 $(2 \times 0.25 = 0.50)$, 2 nickels are worth \$0.10 since each is worth \$0.05 $(2 \times 0.05 = 0.10)$, 1 dime is worth \$0.10, and 4 pennies are worth \$0.04 since each is worth \$0.01. The sum of the coins can be found by writing: $\$0.50 + \$0.10 + \$0.10 + \$0.04$, which equals \$0.74. The sum of the two dollar bills and the coins can be written as: $\$2.00 + \$0.74$. Thus, he paid \$2.74.

4. B: If 1/3 of the balls Wyatt received were basketballs that means the remaining balls he received must have been soccer balls. Since the fraction used is 1/3, look at it as if he received 3 balls. One ball was a basketball and the remaining balls had to be soccer balls. This is now a simple subtraction problem. 3 - 1 = 2 soccer balls.

5. C: The diagram shows 32 counters divided into 4 groups, with 8 counters in each group. Therefore, the total number of counters, 32, is divided by 4, giving a quotient of 8, which is written as: $32 \div 4 = 8$.

6. I, IV,V: All of these statements can represent 6×5 because they all have 6 groups that contain 5 of something. The other two choices represent $6 + 5$.

7. D: The total number of feet he ascended can be determined by adding 482 feet and 362 feet. The sum of 482 and 362 is 844. Thus, he ascended 844 feet in all.

8. C: The item priced at $4.58 can be rounded to $5. The item priced at $6.22 can be rounded to $6. The item priced at $8.94 can be rounded to $9. The sum of 5, 6 and 9 is 20. Thus, the best estimate is $20.

9. B: Choice B shows 4 shaded sections out of 6 total sections. The fraction, $\frac{4}{6}$, is the same as the fraction, $\frac{2}{3}$. Two shaded sections represent one-third of the total. Thus, four shaded sections represent two-thirds of the total. Each of the pictures has 6 total sections, so the other choices can be written as fractions with a 6 in the denominator. Choice A shows $\frac{3}{6}$, which equals $\frac{1}{2}$. Choice C shows . Choice D shows $\frac{2}{6}$, which equals $\frac{1}{3}$. So, only Choice B shows the correct picture.

10. D: A possible first step would be to divide the number of tiles glued each day by the number of hours it took to glue the tiles. The two quotients would then represent approximately how many tiles glued per hour, and could then be compared.

11. Part A: 96: There are 8 guests at the party that each receives 12 tokens. $8 \times 12 = 96$

Part B: 48: If each game requires 2 tokens to play then the number of games that can be played can be found by dividing the total number of tokens by 2. $96 \div 2 = 48$

12. C: Convert the coins to cents and apply addition. Each nickel is worth 5 cents, so 3 nickels equals 15 cents. Each dime is worth 10 cents, so 4 dimes equals 40 cents. Each penny is worth 1 cent, so 2 pennies equals 2 cents. A quarter is worth 25 cents, so 2 quarters equals 50 cents.. 15 + 40 + 2 + 50 = 107 cents. Since there are 100 cents in a dollar, this becomes 1 dollar with 7 cents remaining or $1.07

13. C: Each figure has 3 more squares than the previous figure, so adding 3 to the number of squares in the previous figure yields the number of squares in the next figure. Thus, he will use 14 squares for Figure 5, 17 squares for Figure 6, 20 squares for Figure7, 23 squares for Figure 8, and 26 squares for Figure 9.

14. C: In order to find the amount donated the following year, you multiply the amount donated the previous year by 3. Thus, the amount donated the second year was $6 ($\$2 \times 3$). The amount donated the third year was $18 ($\$6 \times 3$). The amount donated the fourth year was $54 ($\$18 \times 3$). The amount donated the fifth year was $162 ($\$54 \times 3$).

15. The first answer is 4, because $4 \times 3 = 12$, and this can be found by rearranging the equation to $12 \div 3 =$ ___. The second answer is 6, because $16 - 6 = 10$, and this can be found by rearranging the equation to $16 - 10 =$ ___. The last answer is 9, because $8 + 9 = 17$,and this can be found by rearranging the equation to$17 - 8 =$ ___.

16. D: Each spider has 8 legs. In order to find the number of legs present with 3 spiders, you multiply 3 by 8, which is 24. Thus, 3 spiders have 24 legs in all. Choice D is the only table that shows each number of spiders, multiplied by 8, to yield the correct product representing the total number of legs.

17. C: Each candy jar has 14 pieces of candy. This can be determined by dividing the number of pieces of candy by the number of candy jars: $28 \div 2 = 14, 56 \div 4 = 14, 70 \div 5 = 14, 126 \div 9 = 14$. Since the data in the table shows that there are 14 pieces of candy in each jar, multiplying $13 \times 14 = 182$ finds the total number of pieces of candy that are in 13 candy jars.

18. D: If she drinks 8 glasses of water each day, the number of glasses of water she drinks in 12 days can be determined by multiplying 8 by 12. This product is 96; thus she drinks 96 glasses of water in a 12-day time span. The relationship between the number of glasses of water she drinks per day and the total number of glasses of water she drinks in 12 days can be represented by an appropriate multiplication or division number sentence within the following fact family: $8 \times 12 = 96, 96 \div 8 = 12, 12 \times 8 = 96, 96 \div 12 = 8$. Subtracting 8 from 12 will not reveal the number of glasses she drinks in a 12-day time span. The number sentence: $12 - 8 = ?$, is not in this fact family.

19. The answer should look like:

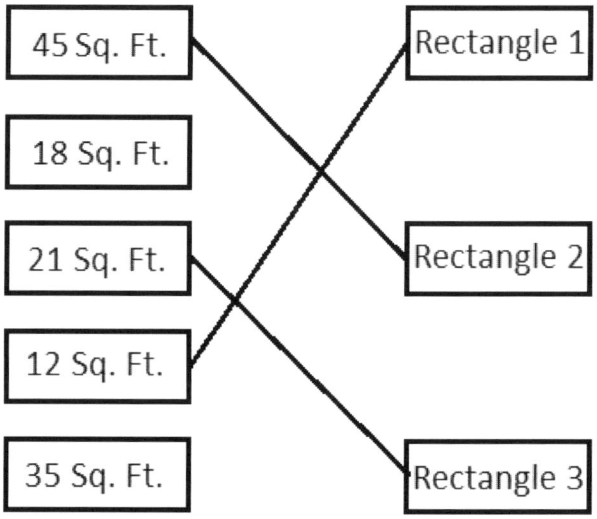

20. D: Choices A, B, and C are all the same right triangle just flipped around. Answer choice D is a different triangle and therefore not congruent.

21. D: 12 ¼ is represented by the first tick mark to the right of the 12. 12 ½ is the second tick mark and 12 ¾ is the third tick mark, or the tick mark before the 13. Only 12 ¾ appears to the right of point M on the number line, making it greater.

22. D: An edge is the intersection of two faces. A triangular pyramid (Choice A) has 6 edges, while a triangular prism (Choice B) has 9 edges, a square pyramid (Choice C) has 8 edges, and a cube (Choice D) has 12 edges. The cube is the only figure with more than 9 edges.

23. C: A vertex is a point where two or more edges meet. A triangle has 3 vertices. Two times that would be 6 vertices. The figure shown for Choice C is a triangular prism, which is the only figure that has 6 vertices. A triangular pyramid (Choice A) has 4 vertices, a cube (Choice B) has 8 vertices, and a square pyramid (Choice D) has 5 vertices.

24. III, V : A face of a shape is each individual surface. Only a cube and a rectangular prism have 6 faces.

25. D: The trapezoid shown for Choice D is congruent to the given shape, provided. Basically, the shapes must be the same size to be congruent, but can be flipped or rotated in any way.

26. Part A: B: Each increment represents one-half. This can be determined by counting that there are 3 marks, or 4 spaces, that lie between the difference of two wholes, as in between 10 and 12. Thus, one increment past 10, where Point P is located, represents $10\frac{1}{2}$.

Part B: A: Point Q is at 9, so the difference between Point P and Point Q is $1\frac{1}{2}$.

27. B: An octagon has 8 lines of symmetry, and 3 lines of symmetry is 5 fewer than 8 lines of symmetry. An equilateral triangle (Choice B) has 3 lines of symmetry, while a square (Choice A) has 4 lines of symmetry, a pentagon (Choice C) has 5 lines of symmetry, and an isosceles trapezoid (Choice D) has 1 line of symmetry. Thus, an equilateral triangle is the only shape shown that has 5 fewer lines of symmetry than an octagon.

28. B: The perimeter is the distance around the figure. So, if you add up all of the numbers you get 22 in.

29. D: The perimeter of the trapezoid is the distance around all of the sides, and is equal to the sum of 3 in, 8 in, 8 in, and 14 in. Thus, the perimeter is 33 in.

30. C: The width of the rectangle is given as 6 in., and the length can be found by multiplying that times 3. $6 \times 3 = 18$

31. C: The trapezoid has 8 square units, plus 4 one-half square units, which equals 2 more square units. The sum of 8 square units and 2 square units is 10 square units.

32. B: The thermometer shows the temperature to be very close to 80 degrees Fahrenheit. It also shows the temperature in Celsius: about 25 degrees.

33. C: The short hand, or hour hand, is between 6 o'clock and 7 o'clock, revealing that Karen went to the library after 6 o'clock. The long hand, or minute hand, is pointed at the 2. Since the 2 on the clock represents 10 minutes after the hour (since each number shown on the clock represents 5 minutes and $2 \times 5 = 10$), the clock shows that Karen went to the library at 6:10.

34. B: There are 16 small squares in total. This means that for $\frac{5}{8}$ of them to be shaded there would need to be 10 of them shaded.

35. 27: To find out how long it takes Ashley to get ready just add up all of the minutes that she spends doing various activities. $6 + 7 + 12 + 2 = 27$

36. D: Texas has the most zoos because it has 15 zoos, while the other states each have 7 zoos, 4 zoos, and 11 zoos. Also, it can be seen from the graph that the bar representing Texas is much higher than the bars for the other states.

37. D: The more fish there is of a certain color the more likely it is that the color of fish is scooped. With more orange fish than striped fish in the bowl, he is more likely to scoop an orange fish than a striped one. There are equal amounts of striped and blue fish, so one is not more likely than the other. There are more orange fish than blue fish, so he is more likely to scoop an orange fish than a blue one.. Finally, the number of striped and blue fish is the same - so they are equally likely to be scooped compared to each other. Thus, Choice D is the only true statement.

38. D: This answer just breaks down the first equation. It adds all of the 10's places first, then adds all of the 1's places.

39. C: Baseball received 6 votes and basketball received only 2 votes. The difference is 6 - 2 = 4 fewer votes.

40. A: Since each tree represents 2 lawns, the pictograph shows that the number of lawns finished by Company A is equal to 6×2, or 12 lawns, the number of lawns finished by Company B is equal to 9×2, or 18 lawns, the number of lawns finished by Company C is equal to 3×2, or 6 lawns, and the number of lawns finished by Company D is equal to 8×2, or 16 lawns. This is the only pictograph that represents the correct number of lawns.

Practice Test #2

Answers and Explanations

1. C: The term subtracted from means to "take away" and place a minus sign in the equation. Since 5 is being subtracted from 25, write the number 25 first followed by a minus sign and then the number 5. The problem states that this subtraction equals 5, so simply attach this to the end.

2. D: Choice D shows 1 crayon and 3 pencils, indicating that 1 out of 4 of Camille's writing tools were crayons. The other choices are out of either a total of 7 writing tools or 5 writing tools, which cannot be used in a ratio that represents 1 out of 4.

3. D: In order to find out the total number of hot dogs she sold in the two months, the amount sold in each month should be added. The sum of 128 and 117 is 245. Thus, she sold 245 hot dogs during the two months.

4. D: The diagram shows 24 counters total, divided into 3 groups, with 8 counters in each group. Therefore, the total number of counters, 24, is divided by 3. This gives a quotient of 8, which is written as: $24 \div 3 = 8$.

5. I, II, V: $2 \times 3 = 6$, so that makes that I. the same. II and V are both 6 groups of 8, which is the same as 6×8.

6. The first on is 4. To find this rearrange the equation to $28 \div 7 = 4$. The second one is 13. To find this rearrange the equation to $22 - 9 = 13$. The last one is 13. To find this rearrange the equation to $18 - 5 = 13$.

7. A: Since a chicken has 2 feet and a horse has 4 feet, you may multiply the number of chickens found on each farm by 2, and then multiply the number of horses found on each farm by 4. After finding the total number of chicken feet and horse feet on each farm, you can then add the two amounts to find the total number of animal feet on each farm. You can then compare the two values to determine the one that is larger.

8. B: Each model shows a whole, split into 7 sections. This makes the denominator equal to 7 for the fraction representing the shaded section for each. Since the fractions all have the same number on the bottom, the number of shaded sections can be compared. For a fraction to be more than $\frac{4}{7}$, more than 4 parts must be shaded. The model shown for Choice B shows the fraction $\frac{6}{7}$, because 6 out of 7 sections are shaded, showing a fraction that is more than 4 out of 7. The other choices all show either 4 parts or less than 4 parts shaded.

9. B: The sequence of the number of miles walked in order from greatest to least is: 963 (Year 4), 691 (Year 1), 567 (Year 2), 221 (Year 5), 144 (Year 3). The number of miles walked can also be compared by examining only the digits in the hundreds place since they are all different. 9 is greater than 6 which is greater than 5 and so on. The only choice that shows the years for the number of miles walked in descending order is B.

10. D: 23 + 12 + 34 = 69. Since the 9 in the ones digit is greater than or equal to five, the number is rounded up to 70.

11.I and IV: To find the answer reduce the fractions to their lowest terms. For the first one, $\frac{4}{6}$, both the numerator and denominator can be divided by 2 to get $\frac{2}{3}$. For the fourth one, $\frac{10}{15}$, both the numerator and the denominator can be divided by 5 to get $\frac{2}{3}$.

12. II and III: To figure out which one is bigger first you need to find a common denominator. The least common denominator of 6 and 8 is 24. So, convert $\frac{5}{8}$ to $\frac{15}{24}$, and $\frac{5}{6}$ to $\frac{20}{24}$, and you see that $\frac{5}{6}$ is bigger. The $\frac{3}{4}$ can just be converted to $\frac{6}{8}$, and you can see that it is bigger than $\frac{5}{8}$.

13. B: The farmer plants 17 rows of corn each season. This can be found using all of the information given in the table. The farmer had planted 34 rows of corn by the end of Season 2 and 68 rows of corn by the end of Season 4, indicating an increase of 34 rows of corn between the two seasons. So, by dividing 34 by 2, the numbers of rows planted in one season is found. Also, the farmer had planted 102 rows of corn by the end of Season 6 and 119 rows of corn by the end of Season 7, indicating an increase of 17 rows of corn planted in one season. If 17 rows of corn are added to the number given at the end of Season 2, the result is 51 rows of corn planted by the end of Season 3. If another 17 rows of corn are added to this amount, the farmer would have planted 68 ears of corn by the end of Season 4, which he did. Thus, he did plant 17 rows of corn each year. He had planted 136 rows of corn by the end of Season 8, 153 rows of corn by the end of Season 9, and 170 rows of corn by the end of Season 10.

14. 35 cm: To find the area of a rectangle just multiply the length times the width.

15. B: A number sentence that subtracts the number of friends from the total number of stamps will not provide the number of stamps needed to give each friend. Instead, an appropriate multiplication or division number sentence within the following fact family is needed: $9 \times 5 = 45$, $5 \times 9 = 45$, $45 \div 9 = 5$, or $45 \div 5 = 9$.

16. D: The number of books brought by 2 students is 8, while the number of books brought by 5 students and 6 students increased by 4. Thus, the number of books brought by each student was 4. This fact can be checked by starting with 1 student and 4 books brought, and continuing the pattern to make sure it corresponds with the numbers in the table. For example, 8 students brought 32, which does in fact agree with the each student bringing 4 books. So, the number of books each student brought, 4, is multiplied by the number of students to find the total number of books that were brought. Thus, 12 students brought 12×4 books, or 48 books.

17. A: A vertex is a point where two or more edges meet. So, a triangular prism (Choice A) has 6 vertices, while a square pyramid (Choice B) has 5 vertices, a triangular pyramid (Choice C) has 4 vertices, and a cube (Choice D) has 8 vertices. Thus, the triangular prism is the only figure with 6 vertices.

18. D: A line of symmetry is a line that can be drawn through a shape such that the remaining part of the shape on either side of the line looks the same, but is reflected. The shape shown is a hexagon, and it has 6 lines of symmetry. An octagon (Choice D) has 8 lines of symmetry, while an equilateral triangle (Choice A) has 3 lines of symmetry, a rhombus (Choice B) has 2 lines of symmetry, and a trapezoid (Choice C) has 1 line of symmetry. So, the only shape with more lines of symmetry than the hexagon is the octagon.

19. Each tick mark on the number line represents a change of $\frac{1}{4}$. The number line below shows the correct placement of the point.

20. B: The figure shown is a square pyramid. It indeed has 5 vertices and 5 faces. It has 8 edges, not 6 edges, so Choice B is the only statement that is not true.

21. 185: She starts with 152 stickers and then gives 34 away. So, 152-34=118. Then she buys 67 more, which gives her 118+67=185.

22. A: A triangular pyramid (Choice A) has 4 faces, while a triangular prism (Choice B) and a rectangular pyramid (Choice D) both have 5 faces. A cube (Choice C) has 6 faces. Thus, the only figure with less than 5 faces is the triangular pyramid.

23. D: Figures A, B, and C can all be folded in a manner that the squares lay directly on top of each other. This cannot be done with Figure D; therefore, Figure D does not have a line of symmetry.

24. Part A: C: If you count all of the boxes you see that the figure is divided into 11 pieces.

Part B: C: Now count the boxes that are shaded in and you get 6, so $\frac{6}{11}$ are shaded.

25. B: The area of a rectangle is found by multiplying length times width. In this problem you are given the area and the width and asked to find length *x*. To find this divide 36 by 4 to get 9.

26. B: The perimeter is the sum of the lengths of all five sides, or $5 + 5 + 3 + 3 + 4$, which equals 20. Therefore, the perimeter of the pentagon is 20 cm.

27. B: To find the perimeter of each shape, add up the lengths of all of the sides. The square has four sides of equal length, so it has a perimeter of 16 centimeters, which is larger than the perimeters of the other three shapes. The triangle and rectangle each have a perimeter of 14 centimeters. The hexagon has a perimeter of 12 centimeters.

28. Part A: 180: To find the total number of minutes he reads multiply 6 times 30 to get 180.

Part B: 3: An hour is 60 minutes, so if takes 180 and divide by 60 to get 3.

29. B: The total weight of the watermelons was 28, and if each one weighed the same then you can just divide by 7 to get 4 pounds each.

30. D: The triangle includes 21 whole square units, plus 7 one-half square units, or $3\frac{1}{2}$ square units. So, 21 square units plus $3\frac{1}{2}$ square units gives a total of $24\frac{1}{2}$ square units.

31. Part A: 32cm: The perimeter of a rectangle is the length of all of the sides added together. The length is 9 and the width is 7, but there are two lengths and two widths, so $7 + 7 + 9 + 9 = 32$ cm.

Part B: 63 cm: The area of a rectangle id length times width, so $7 \times 9 = 63$.

32. C: To find how much total time John spent walking, add the time together. 9 minutes plus 12 minutes plus 23 minutes equals 44 minutes, $9 + 12 + 23 = 44$. Therefore, John walked for a total of 44 minutes from the time he left his house until he returned home.

33. A: The short hand, or hour hand, is between 10 o'clock and 11 o'clock, revealing that Amanda arrived after 10 o'clock, but before 11 o'clock. It is much closer to the 10, so this indicates the time is much closer to 10 o'clock than 11 o'clock. The long hand, or minute hand, is pointing to the 2, indicating 10 minutes after the hour. This is because for minutes, each number represents 5 minutes; so $2 \times 5 = 10$. So, she arrived at the party at 10:10.

34. B: There are 6 yellow cards and 3 red cards. The more cards there are of a certain color, the more likely it is that the color is drawn. With more yellow cards than red cards in the bag, he is more likely to draw a yellow card than a red card. There are more green cards than yellow cards, so he is more likely to draw a green card than a yellow card. There are less yellow cards than blue cards, so he is less likely to draw a yellow card than a blue card. Finally, the number of red, blue, green, and yellow cards are all different - so none of them are equally likely to be drawn compared to another color. Thus, Choice B is the only true statement.

35. D: Since the spinner only has sections, labeled 1 - 8, there is not a section, labeled "9". Therefore, it is impossible for the spinner to land on a 9.

36. C: The more candy there is of a certain kind, the more likely it is that the candy is drawn. With more lollipops than chocolates in the bowl, she is more likely to draw a lollipop than a chocolate. There are more peppermints than chocolates, so she is more likely to draw a peppermint than a chocolate. There are more peppermints than lollipops, so she is more likely to draw a peppermint than a lollipop. Finally, the number of chocolates, peppermints, and lollipops are all different - so none of them are equally likely to be drawn compared to another color. Thus, Choice C is the only true statement.

37. C: Florida had 20 teachers that attended the event, which is less than the number of teachers who attended the event from each of the other three states. The number of teachers that attended the event from each of the other states were 40 (Arizona), 80 (New York), and 50 (California). Also, just looking at the bar graph shows that Florida had the least number of teachers attend compared to the other states because the bar is much lower in the graph.

38. A: The pictograph for Choice A reveals that each picture of a cake represents 5 actual cakes. Therefore, the numbers given in the table, divided by 5, should equal the number of cakes represented in the pictograph. The pictograph accurately shows 5 cakes for 25 actual cakes, 3 cakes for 15 actual cakes, 7 cakes for 35 actual cakes, and 4 cakes for 20 actual cakes. This is the only pictograph that represents the correct number of cakes.

39. The hamster received 10 votes and the fish received 2 votes. The difference is 10 - 2 = **8 votes**.

40. II and III: $32 - 9 = 23$ is a true statement. Also $\frac{4}{5} = \frac{8}{10}$ is true because 4 and 5 can each be multiplied by 2 to get 8 and 10.

Online Resources

Due to our efforts to try to keep this book to a manageable length, we've created a link that will give you access to all of your online resources:

mometrix.com/resources719/ssnystg3mathwb

It's Your Moment, Let's Celebrate It!

Share your story @mometrixtestpreparation